ARTWORK BY BETH NELSON

traveller

GW00705973

caminante

STEWART, TABORI & CHANG
NEW YORK

Published in 2000 by
STEWART, TABORI & CHANG
A division of U.S. Media Holdings, Inc.
115 West 18th Street • New York, NY 10011

Distributed in Canada by
General Publishing Company Ltd.
30 Lesmill Road
Don Mills, Ontario, Canada M3B 2T6

ISBN 1-58479-001-6

EDITOR • MARISA BULZONE
DESIGNED BY ALEXANDRA MALDONADO
GRAPHIC PRODUCTION BY KIM TYNER

Printed and bound in Hong Kong

10 9 8 7 6 5 4 3 2 1

FIRST PRINTING

"Traveller, there is no path.
Paths are made by walking."

~~04 - 03-01 - 22.33 - 00.35~~

~~LL - 04-01 - 23-40 - 2-10~~

~~LL - 05-01 - 03.30 - 05-15~~

05-01.
~~LL - 23-50 - 01-20~~
~~LL - 06-01 - 02-10 - 03.55~~

~~LL - 06-01 - 23-45 - 01-30~~.

~~LL - 08-01 - 19-15 - 21-00~~.

~~LL - 08-01 - 23-45 - 01-45~~

~~LL - 09-01 - 02-05 - 03.45~~.

~~LL - 09-01 - 21-45 - 23-35~~.

LL - 10-01 - 23.44 - 00 - 44
11-01   00.45 - 01-45

Atlantico

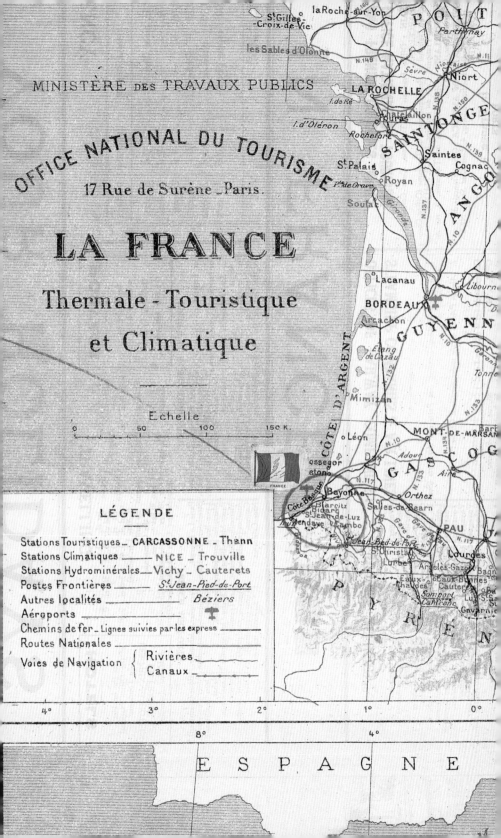

ADIEU, NEW-YORK!

Tra

TRANSATLANTICO

COLUMBIA

VIA
AIR
MAIL

URGENTE

POLVORONES

LA CONCHA

SAN SEBASTIAN

It is sometimes better to travel
hopefully than to arrive.
Lucky Numbers 11, 14, 23, 28, 32, 34

ÆRRITZ

VIA AIR MAIL

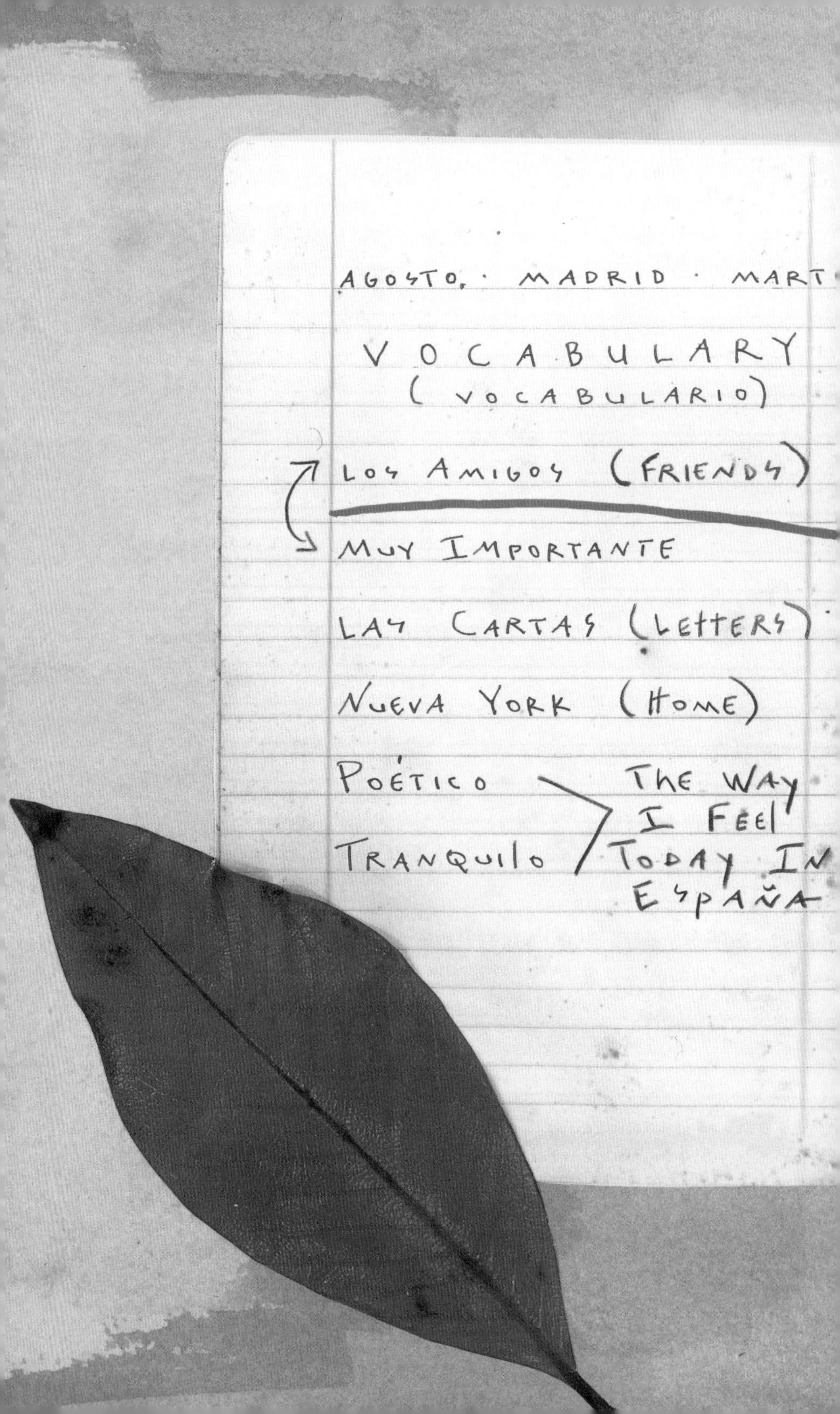

AGOSTO · MADRID · MART

VOCABULARY
(VOCABULARIO)

LOS AMIGOS (FRIENDS)

MUY IMPORTANTE

LAS CARTAS (LETTERS)

NUEVA YORK (HOME)

POÉTICO ⎫ THE WAY
⎬ I FEEL
TRANQUILO ⎭ TODAY IN
ESPAÑA

"Caminante, no hay camino
Se hace camino al andar."

Antonio Machado

Words of weather...

Tormenta

Tempestad *storm*

Tormentoso *stormy*

Viento *wind*

Lluvia *rain*

Esta lloviendo *it is raining*

Nube *cloud*

Nublado *cloudy*

Galerna *wind storm from off the sea,*
found in the north of Spain

MAR CANTABR

SAN SEBASTIA

GUETARIA

DEVA

ZUMAYA

ZARAUZ

ORIO

MENDARO

ALTO DE ICIAR

RIO UROLA

RIO DEVA

RIO

ALZOLA

ELGOIBAR

MALZAGA

TOLOYA

La aventura puede ser
una verdadera felicidad.